Rude Britannia Swear Word Colouring Book

By: Shazza T. Jones

I0465355

Introduction

Learn to swear like a Brit while you sit back and colour the pages.

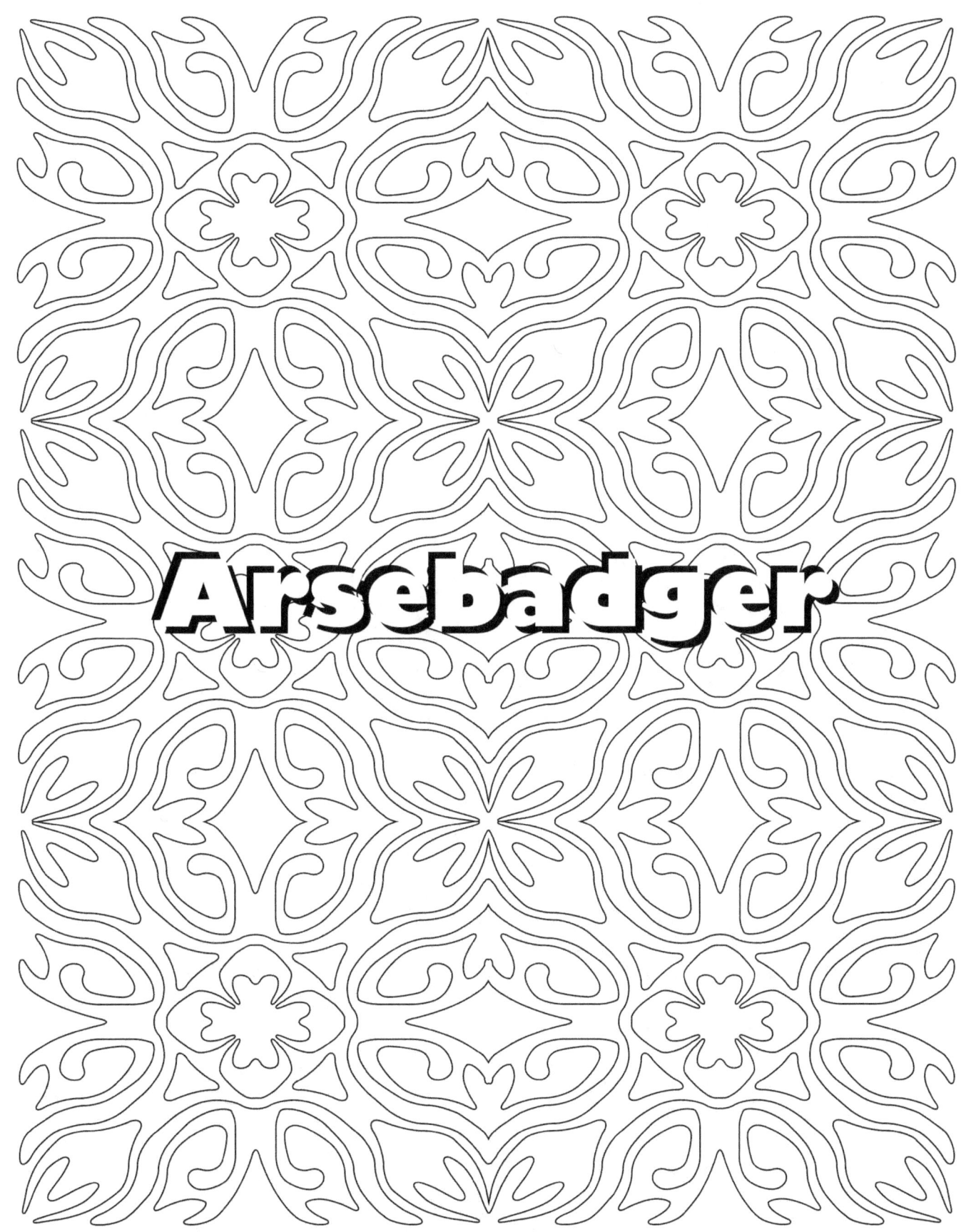

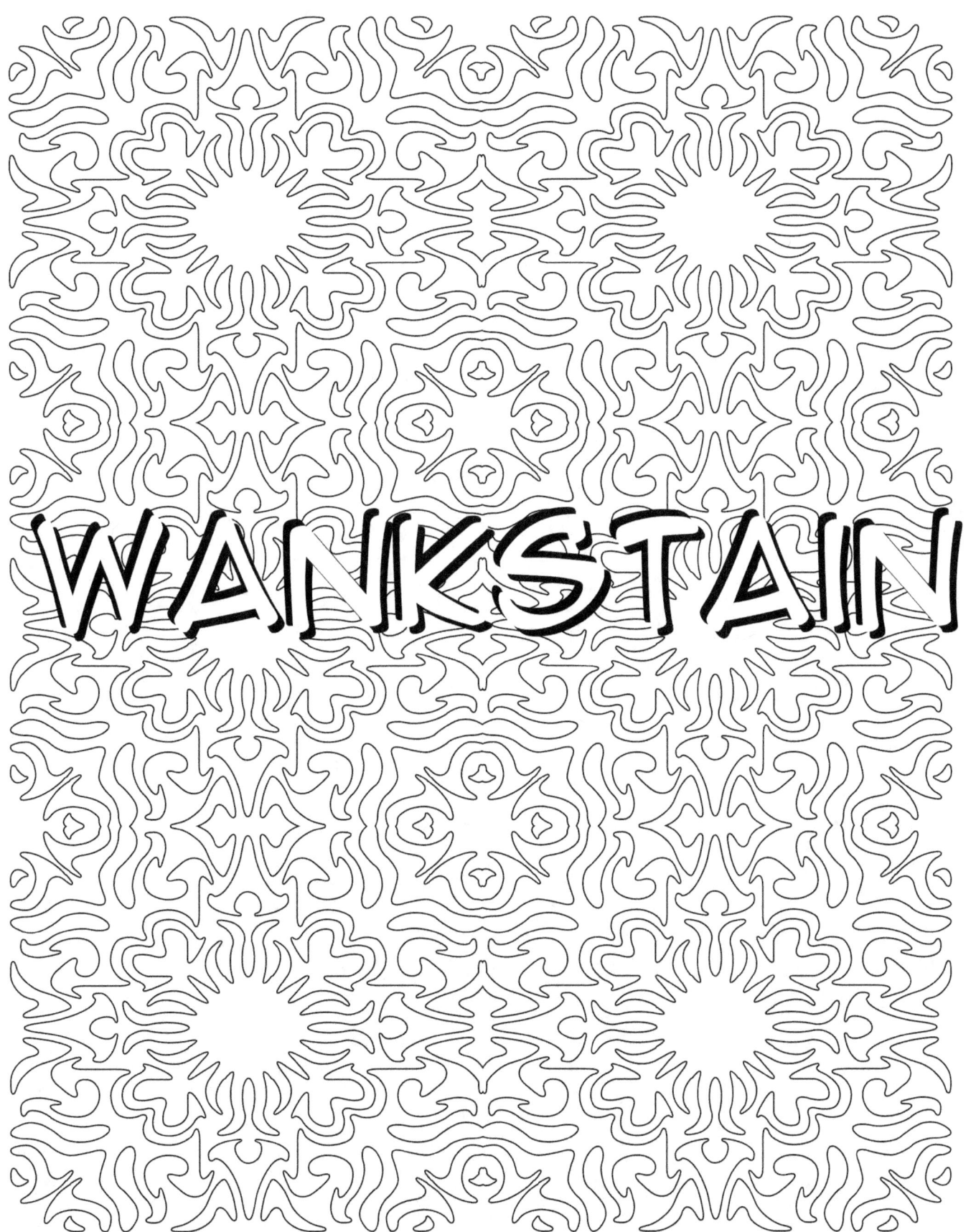

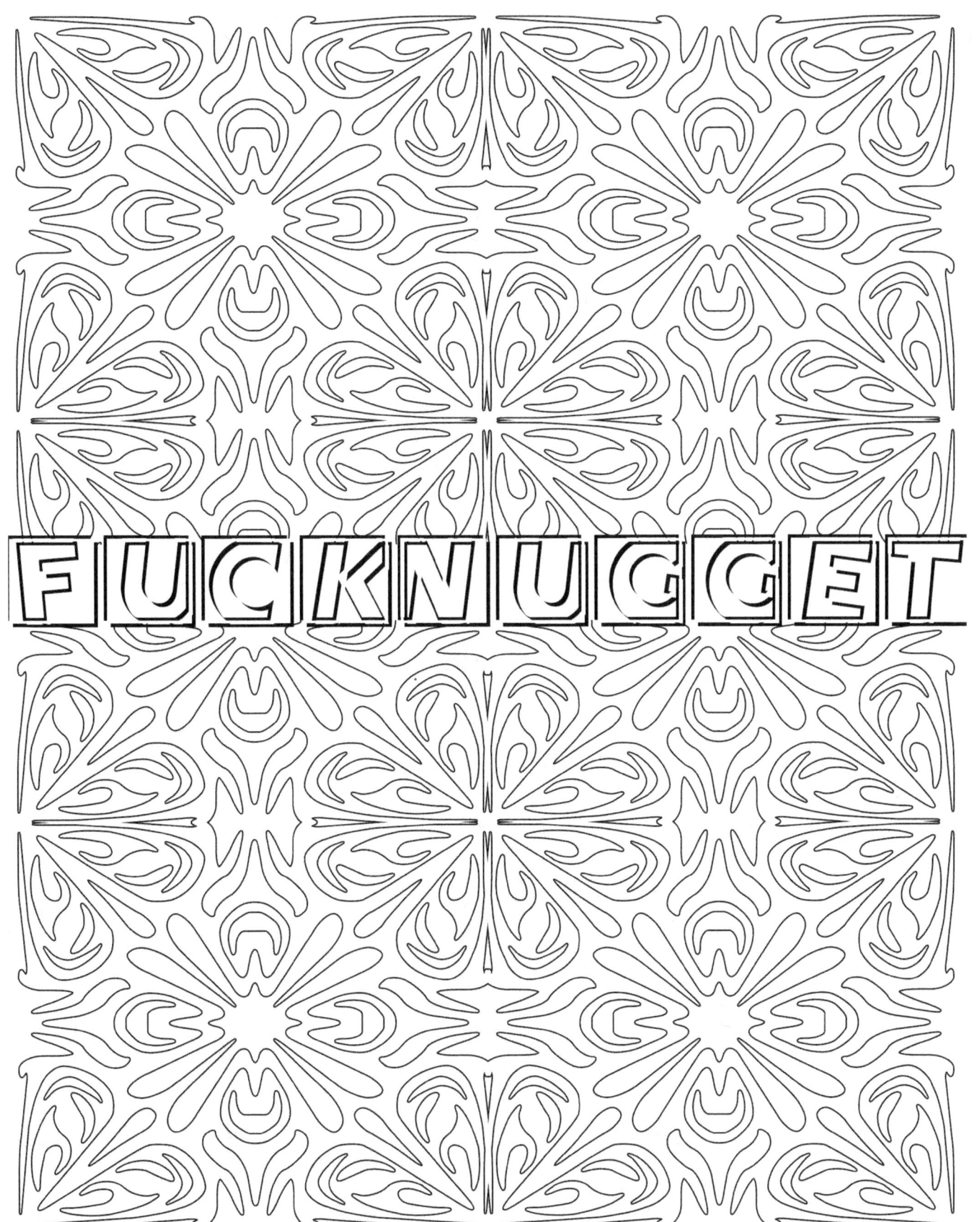

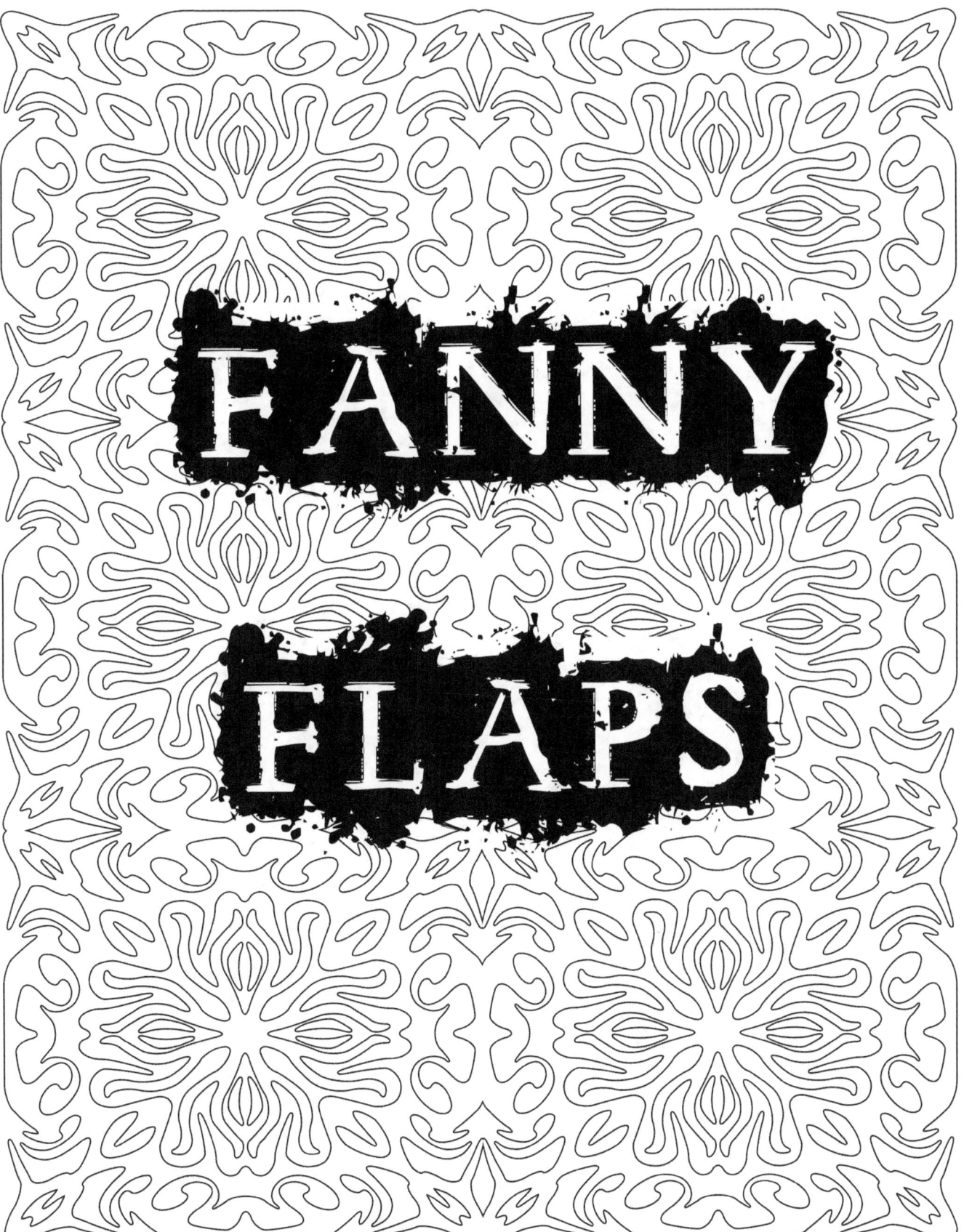

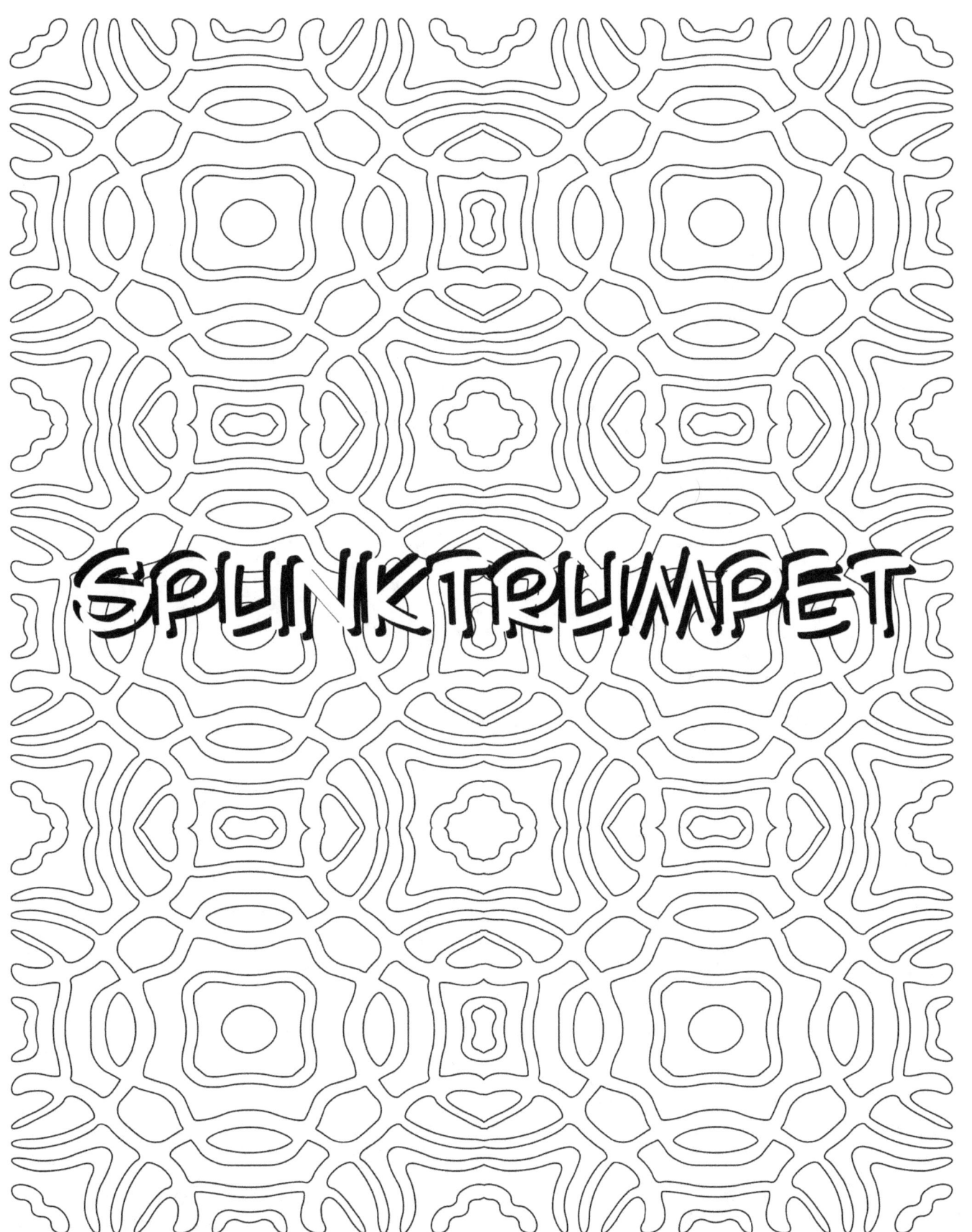

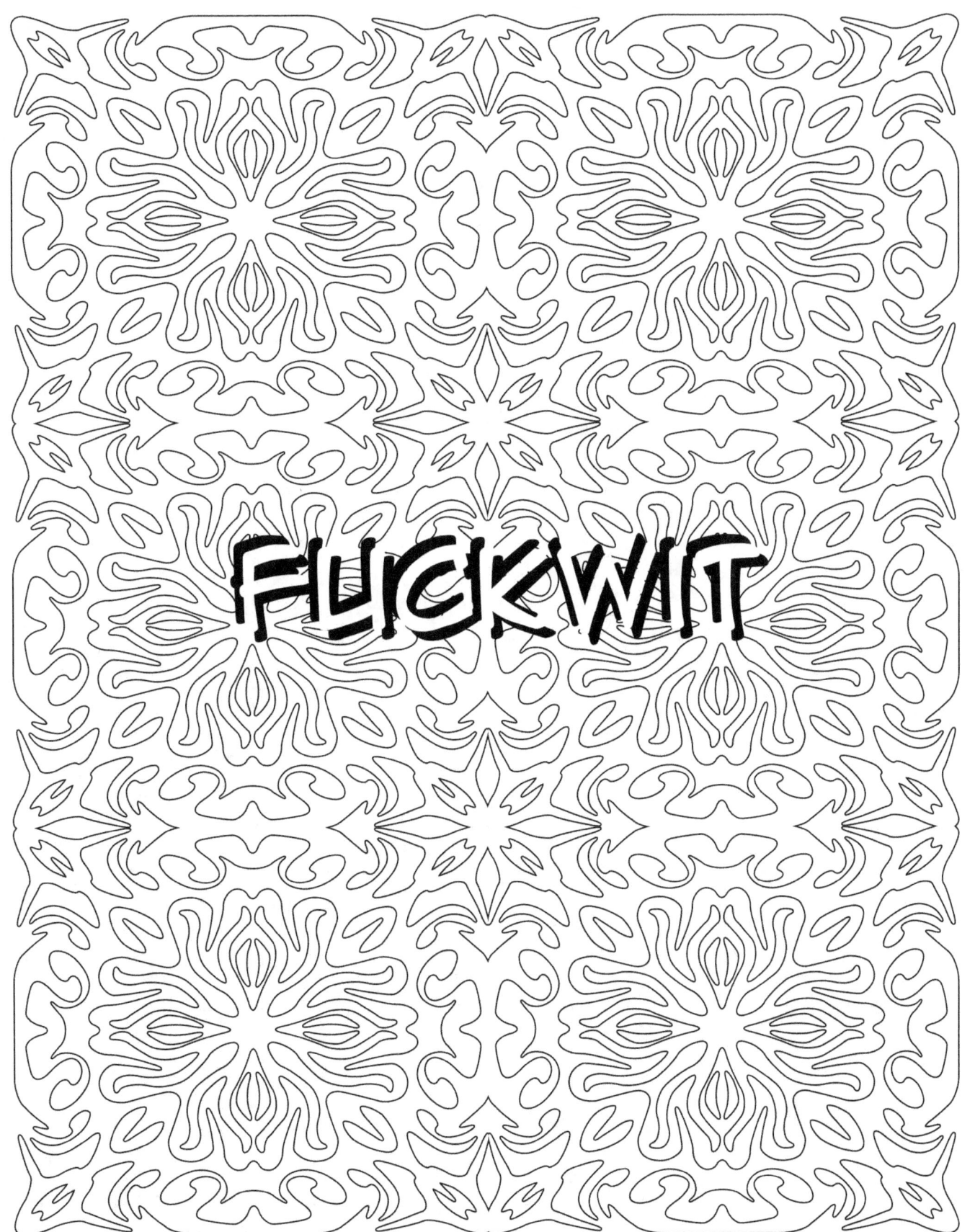

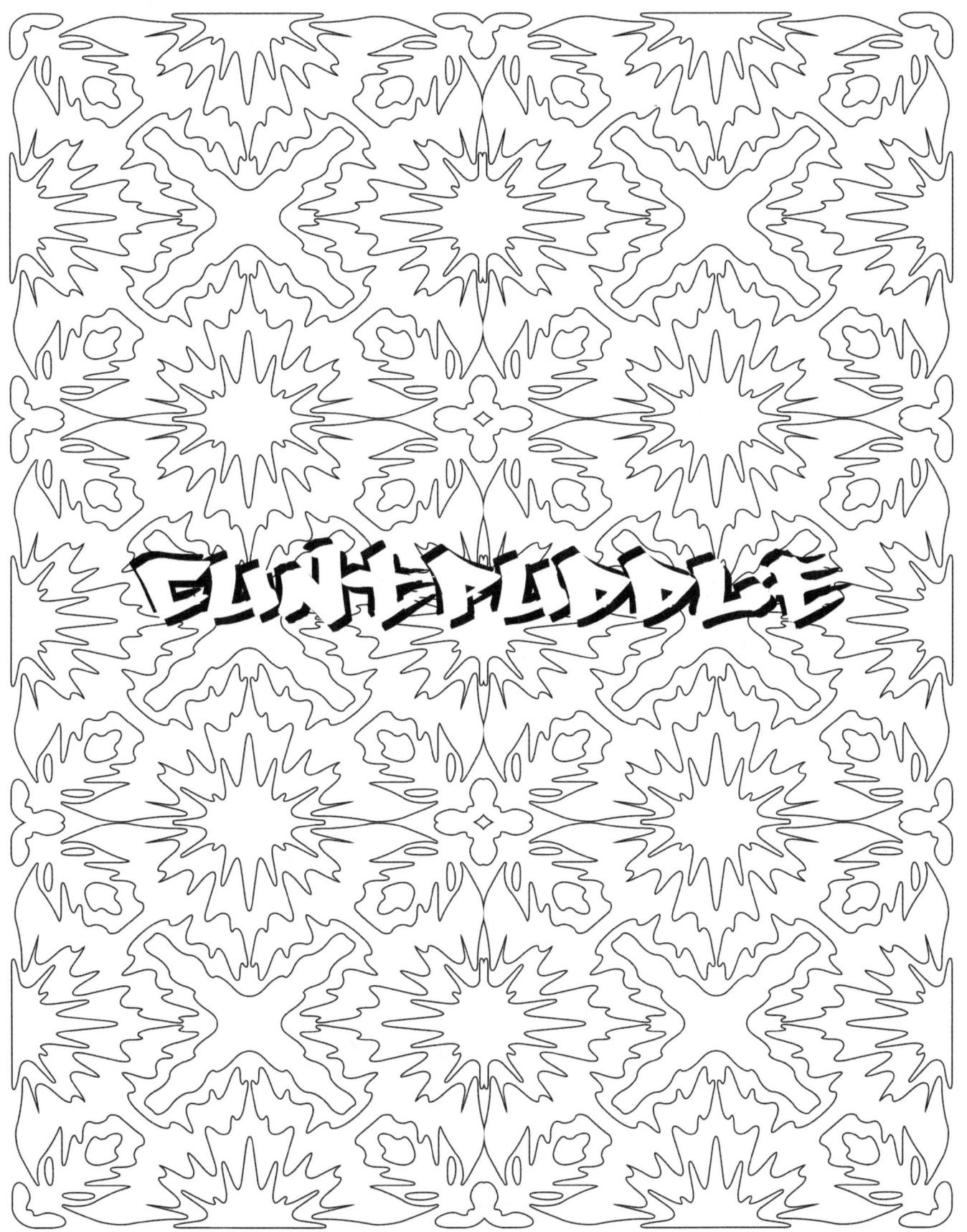

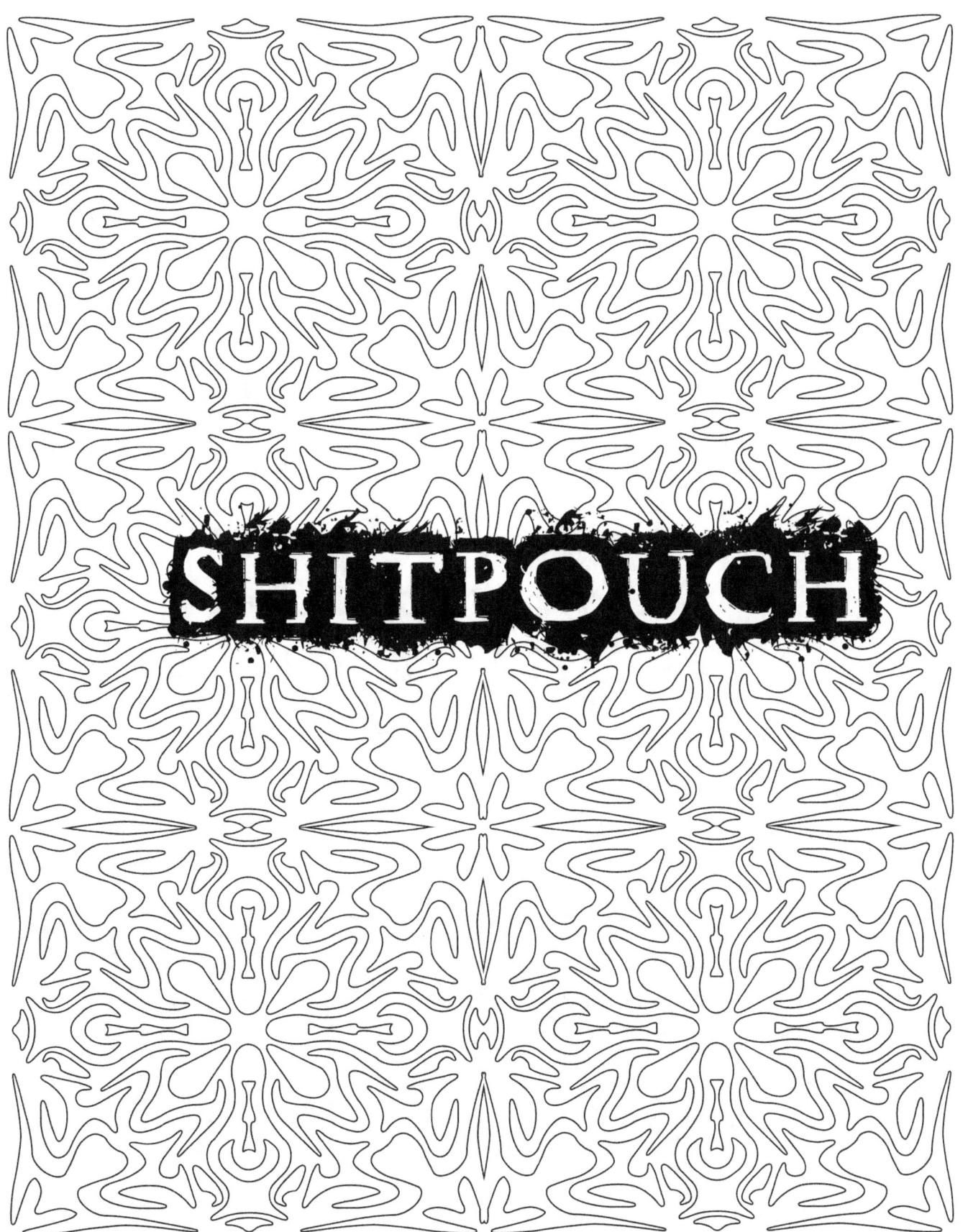

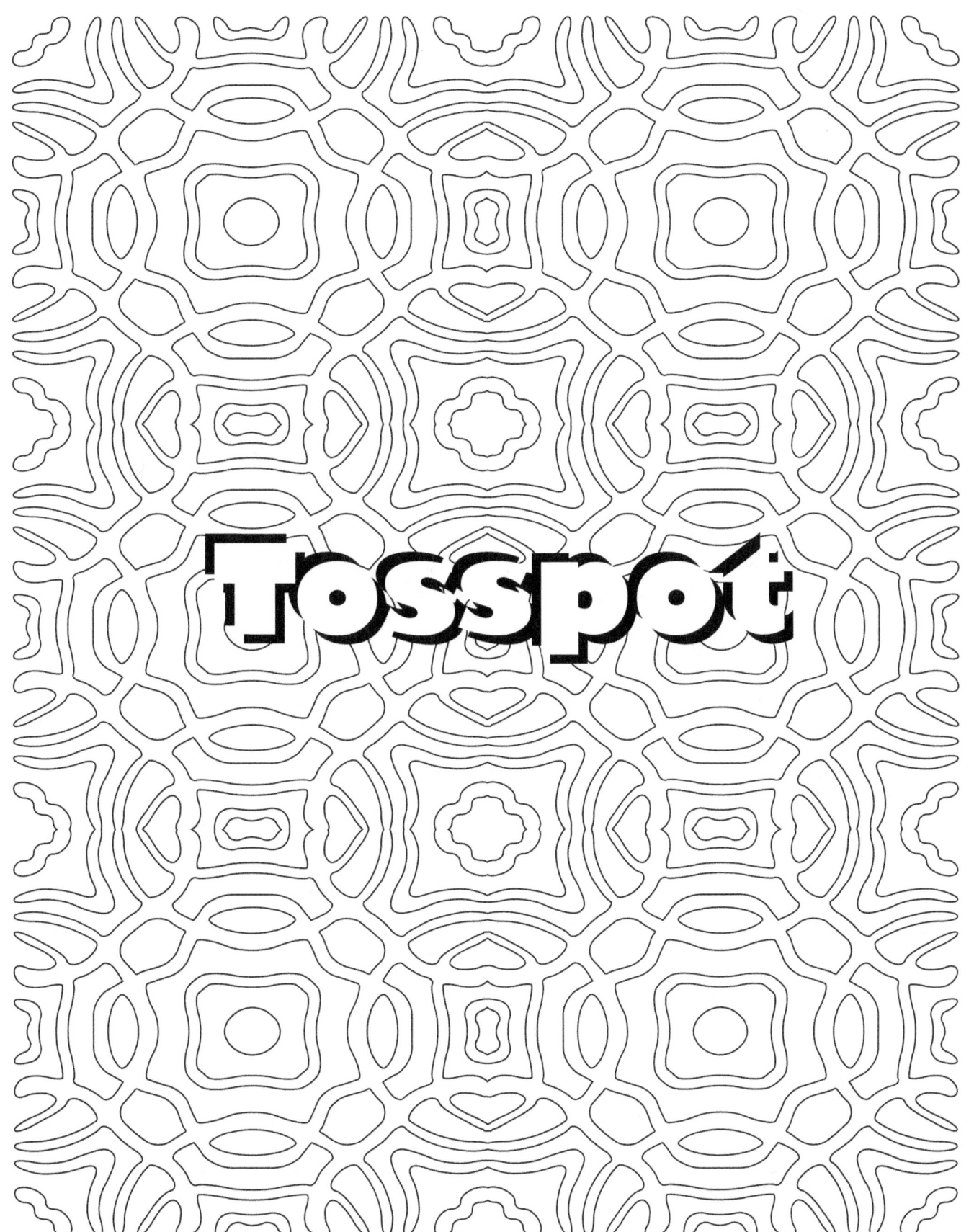

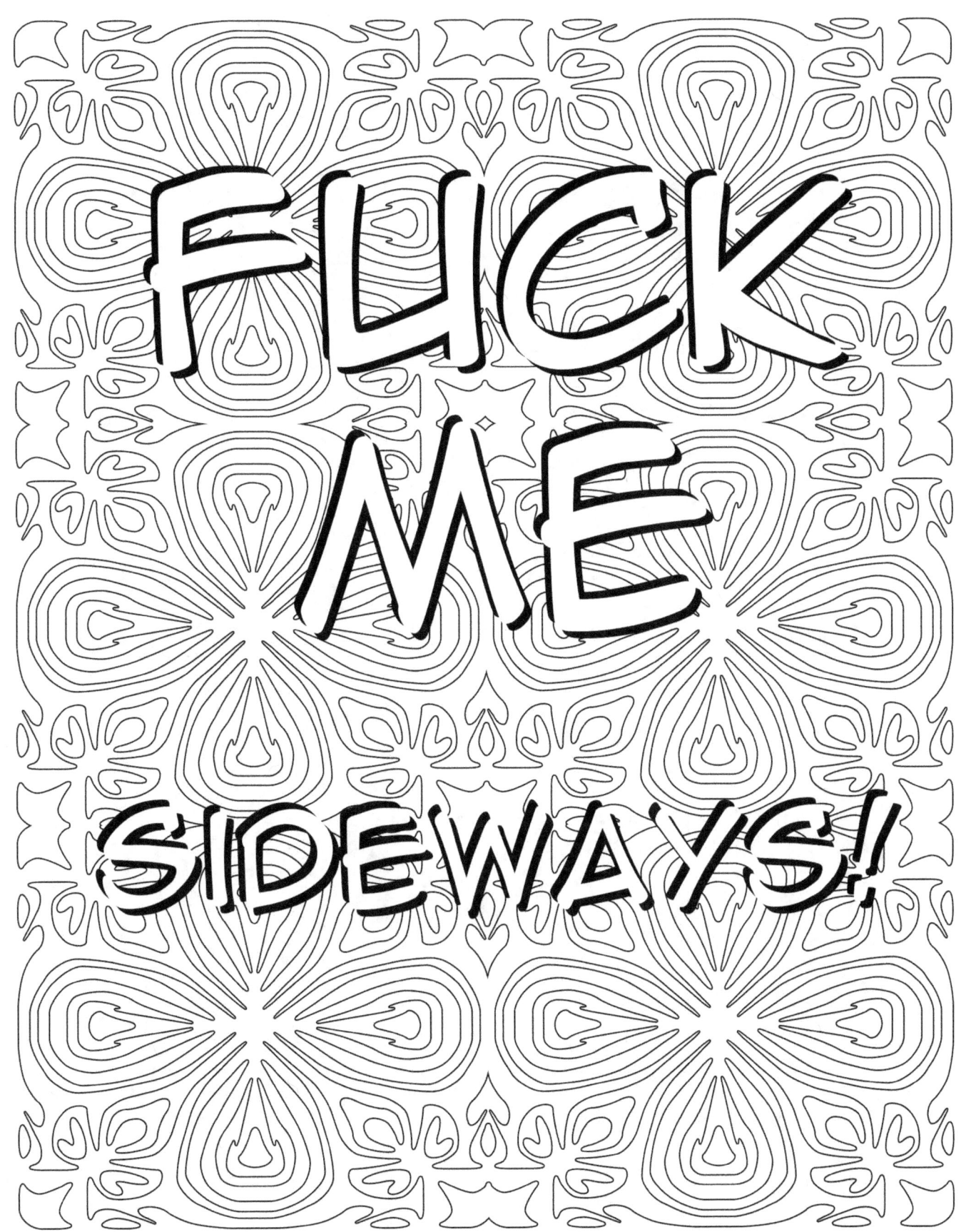

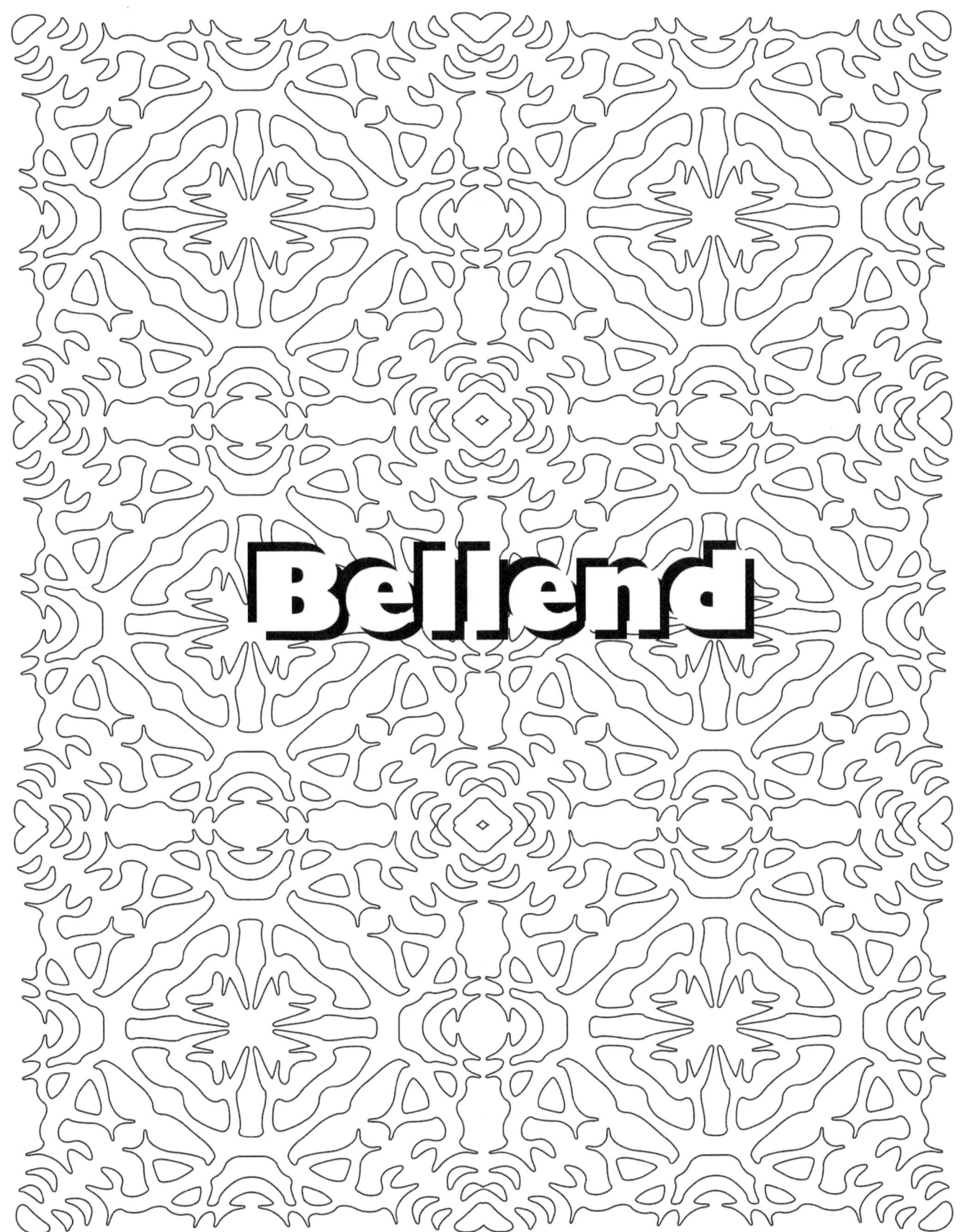

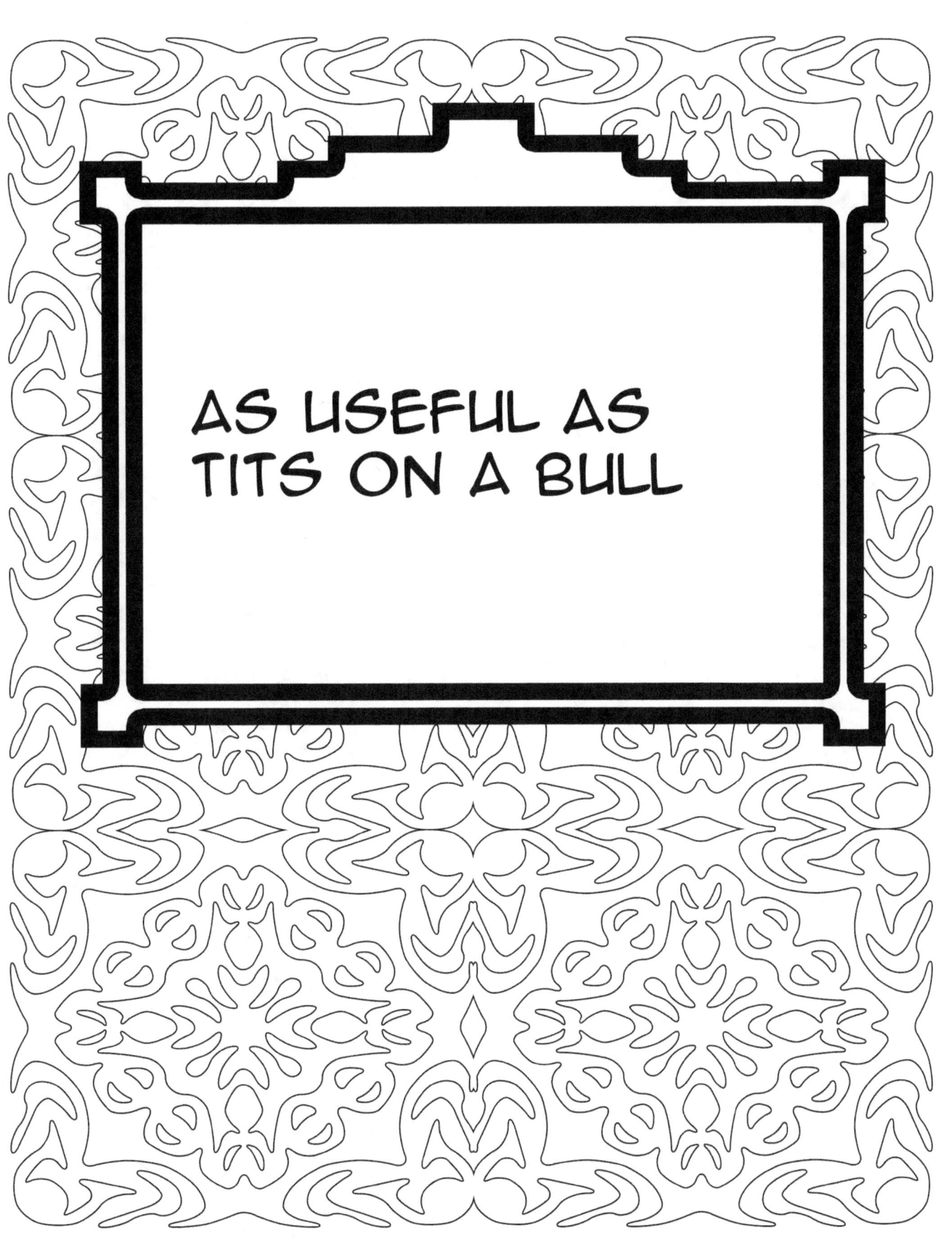

AS USEFUL AS
TITS ON A BULL

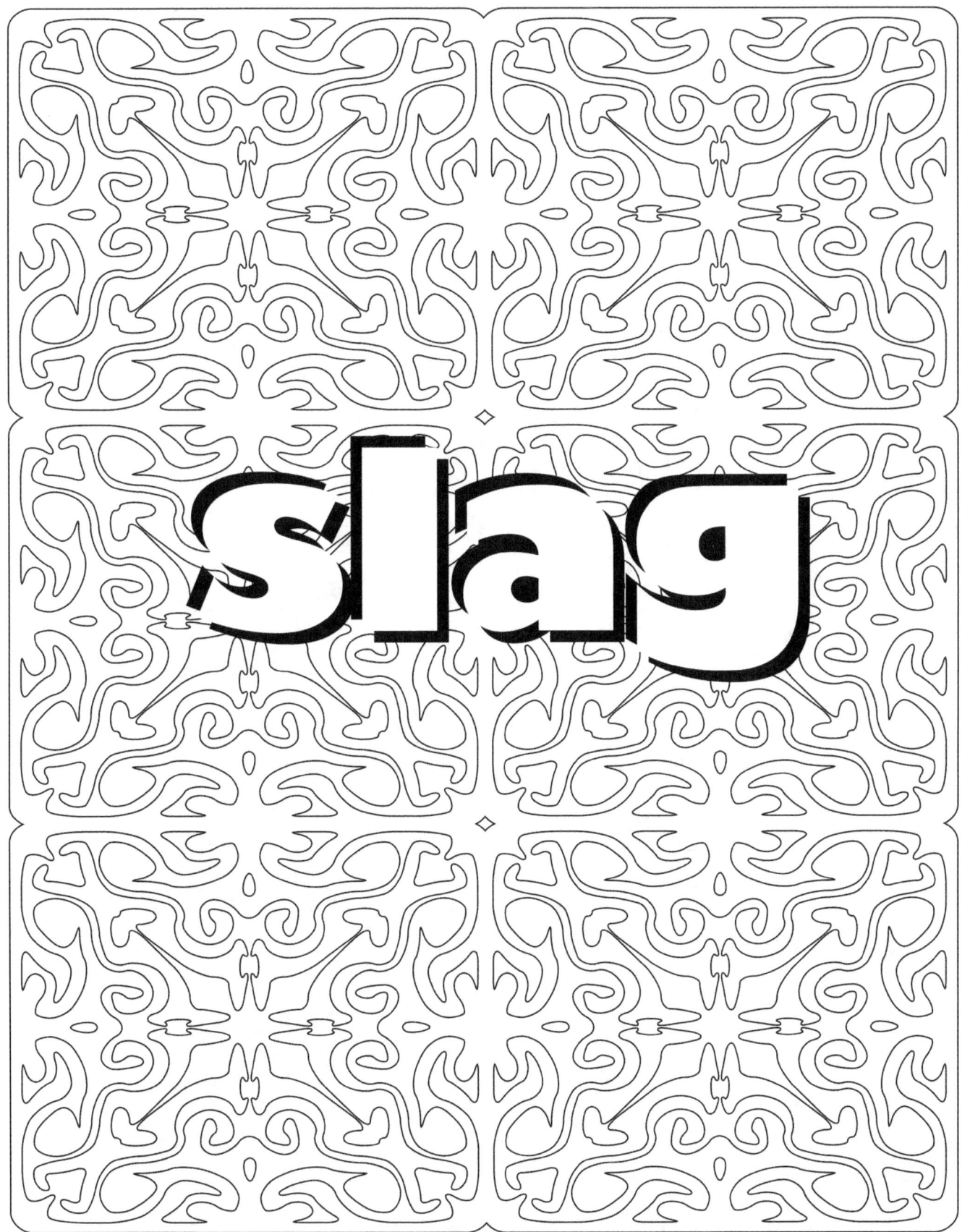

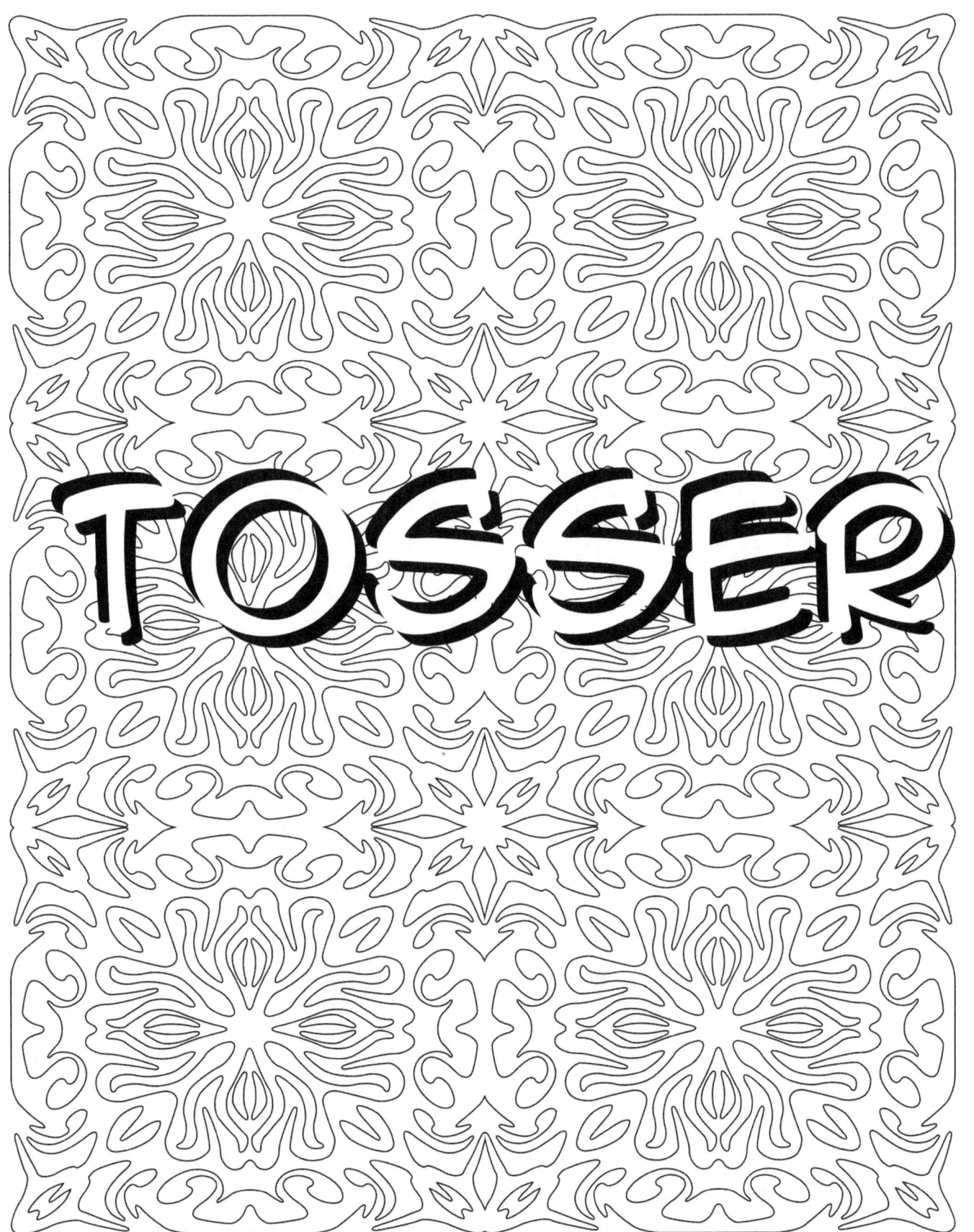

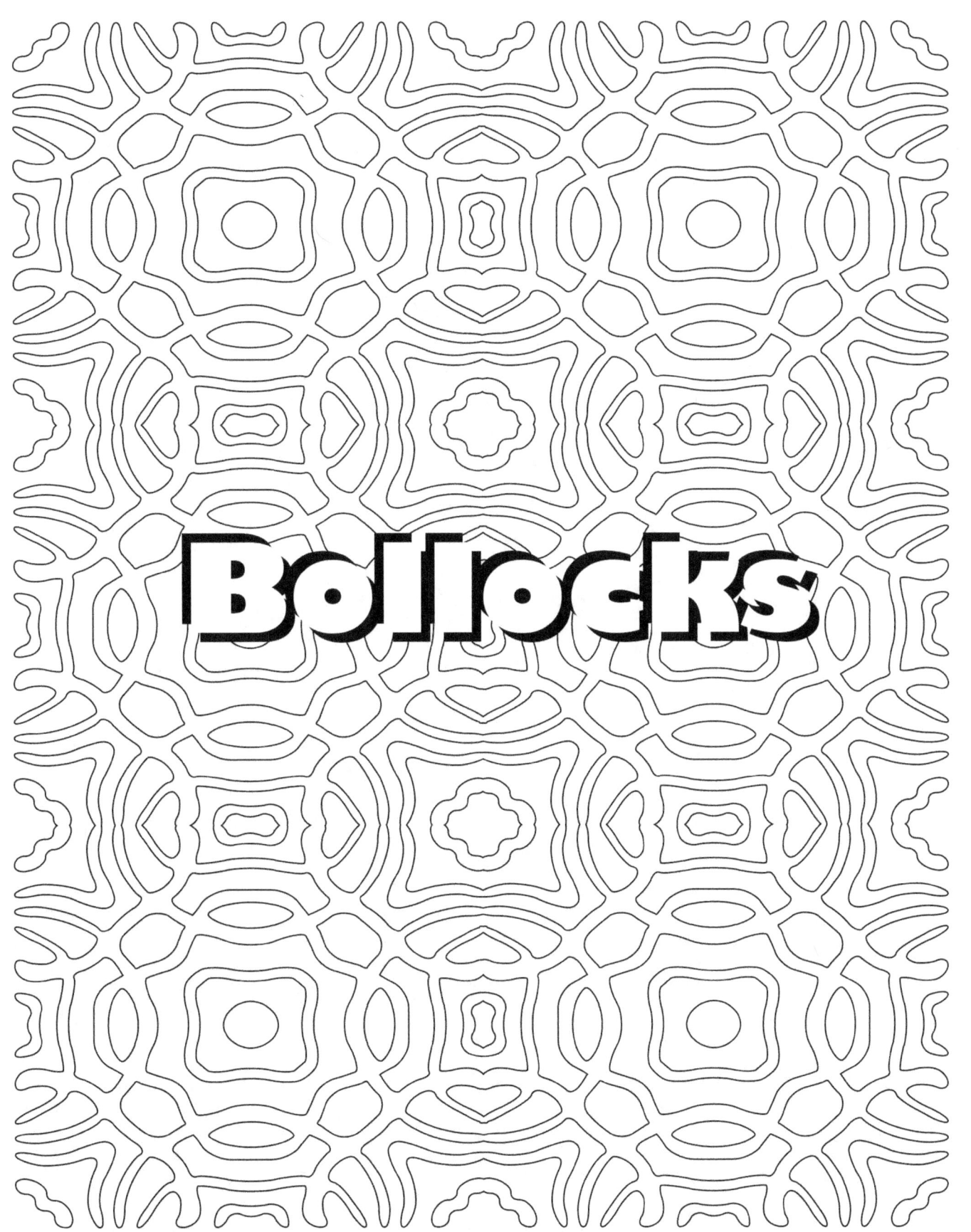

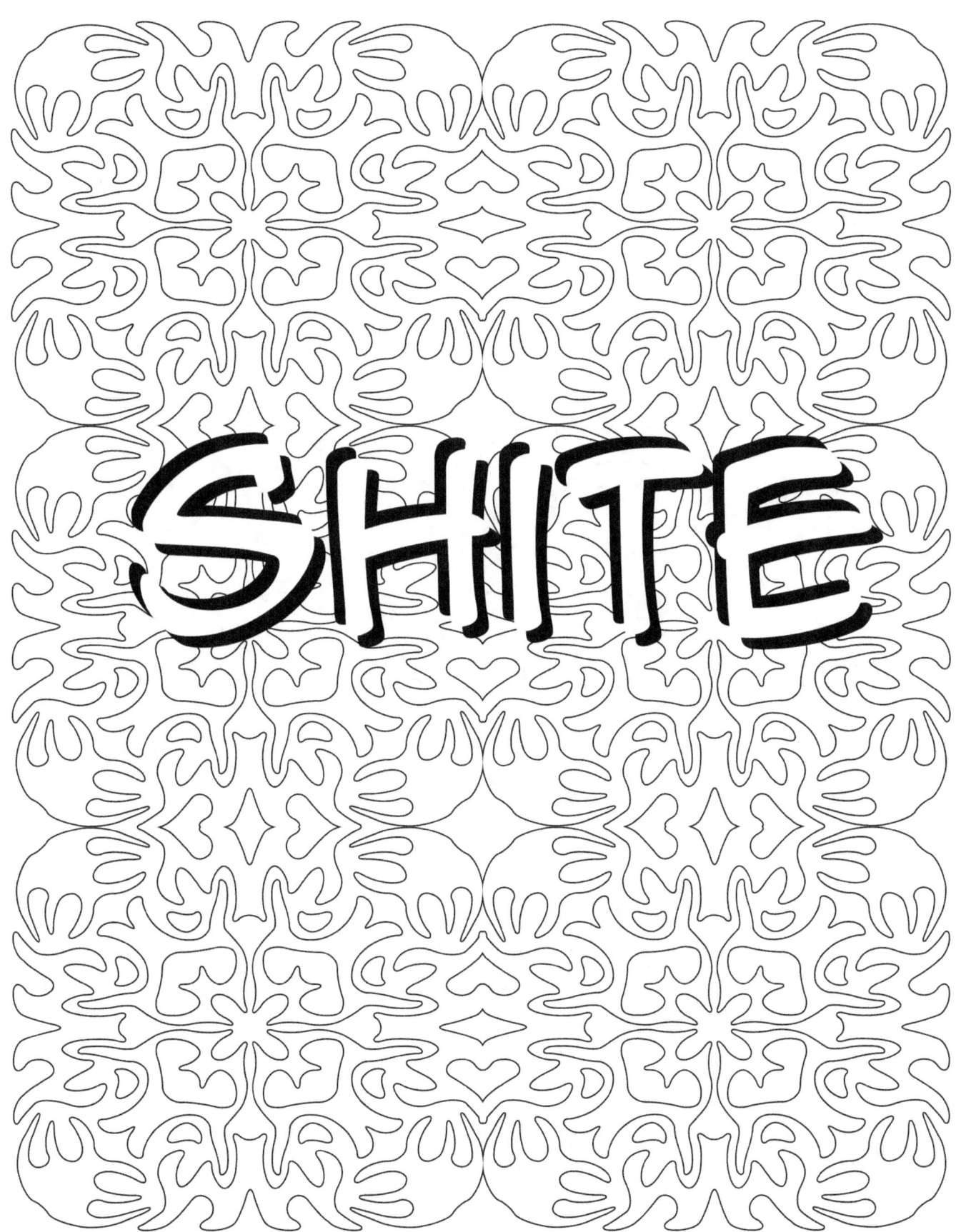

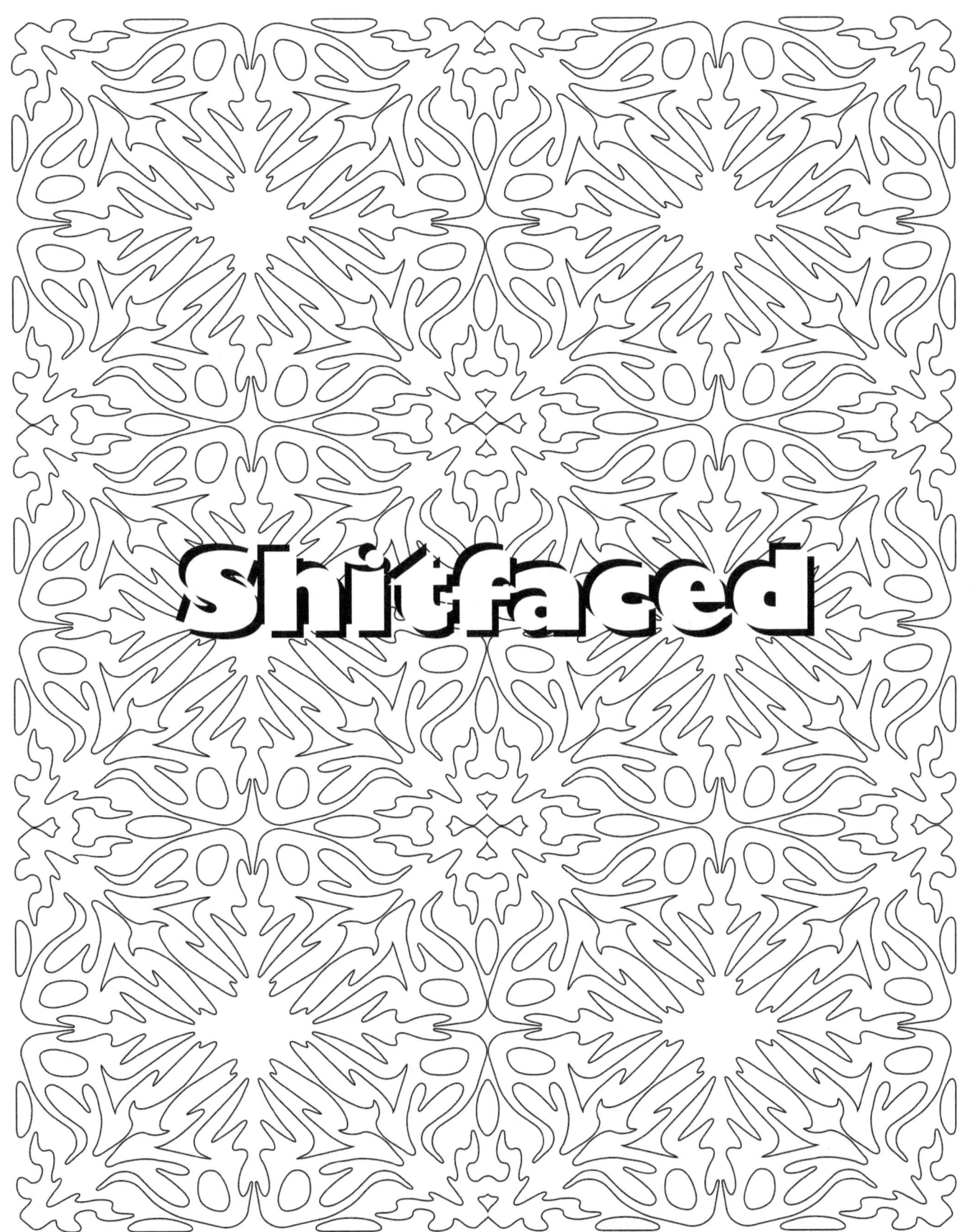

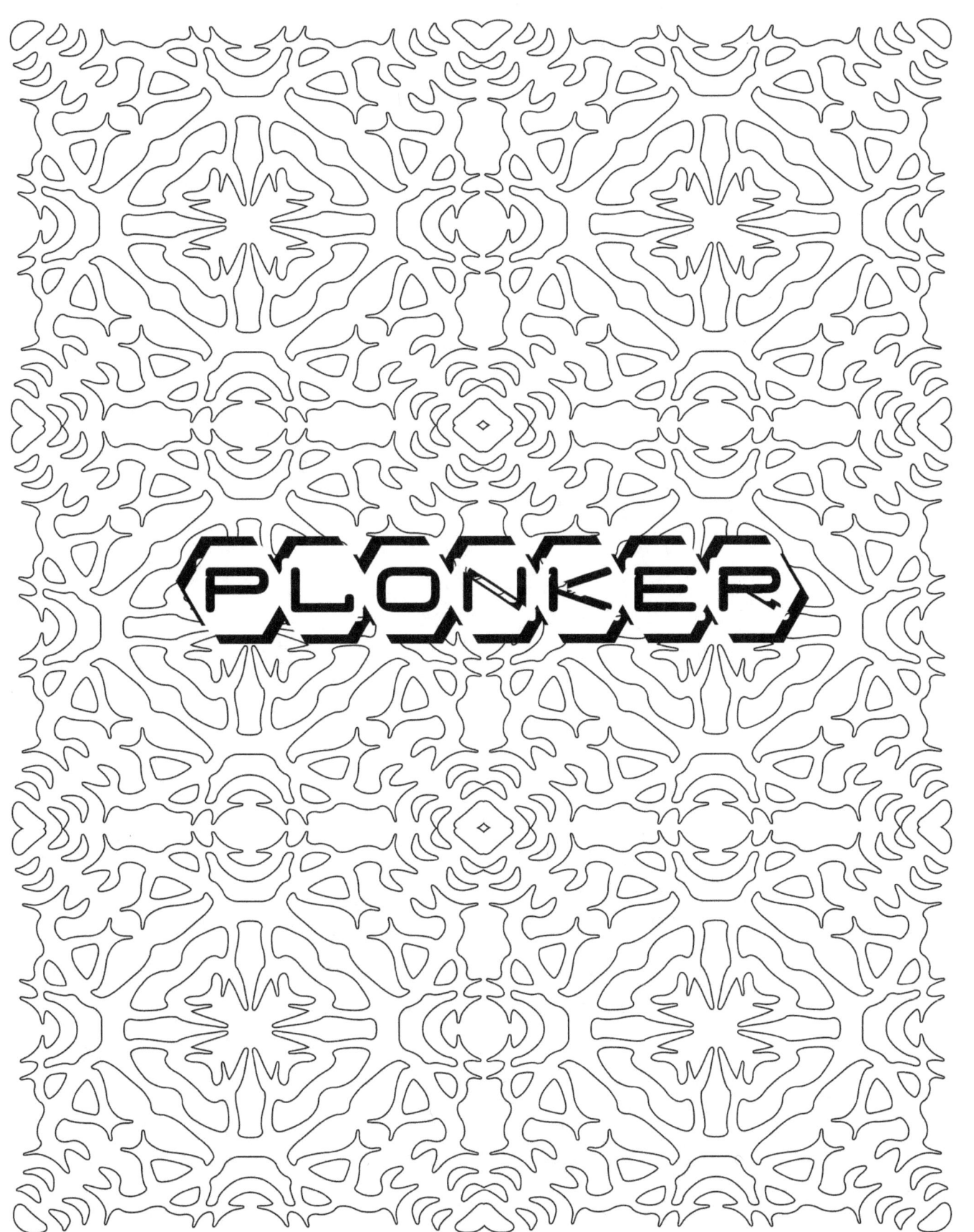

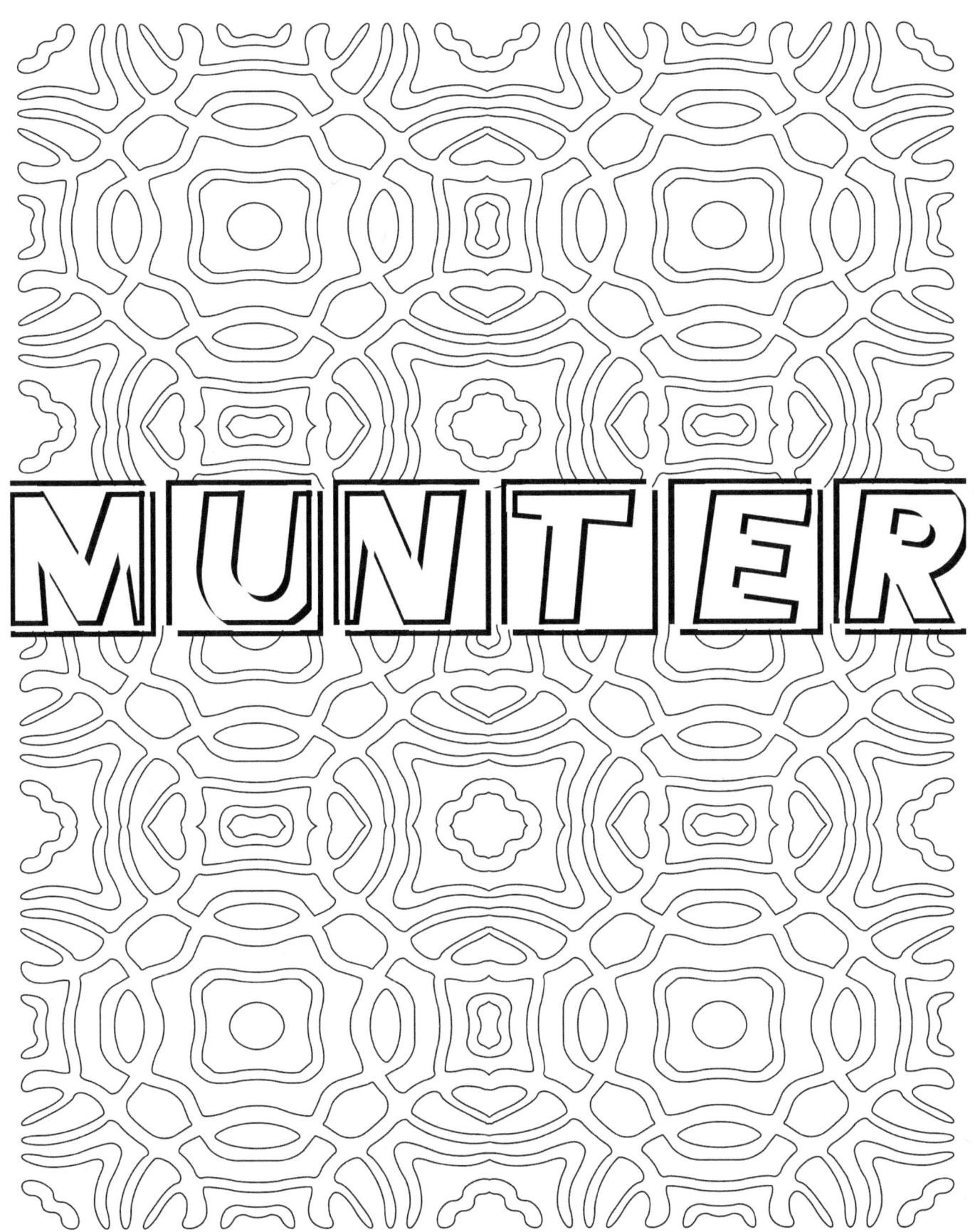

FUCKIN CUNT

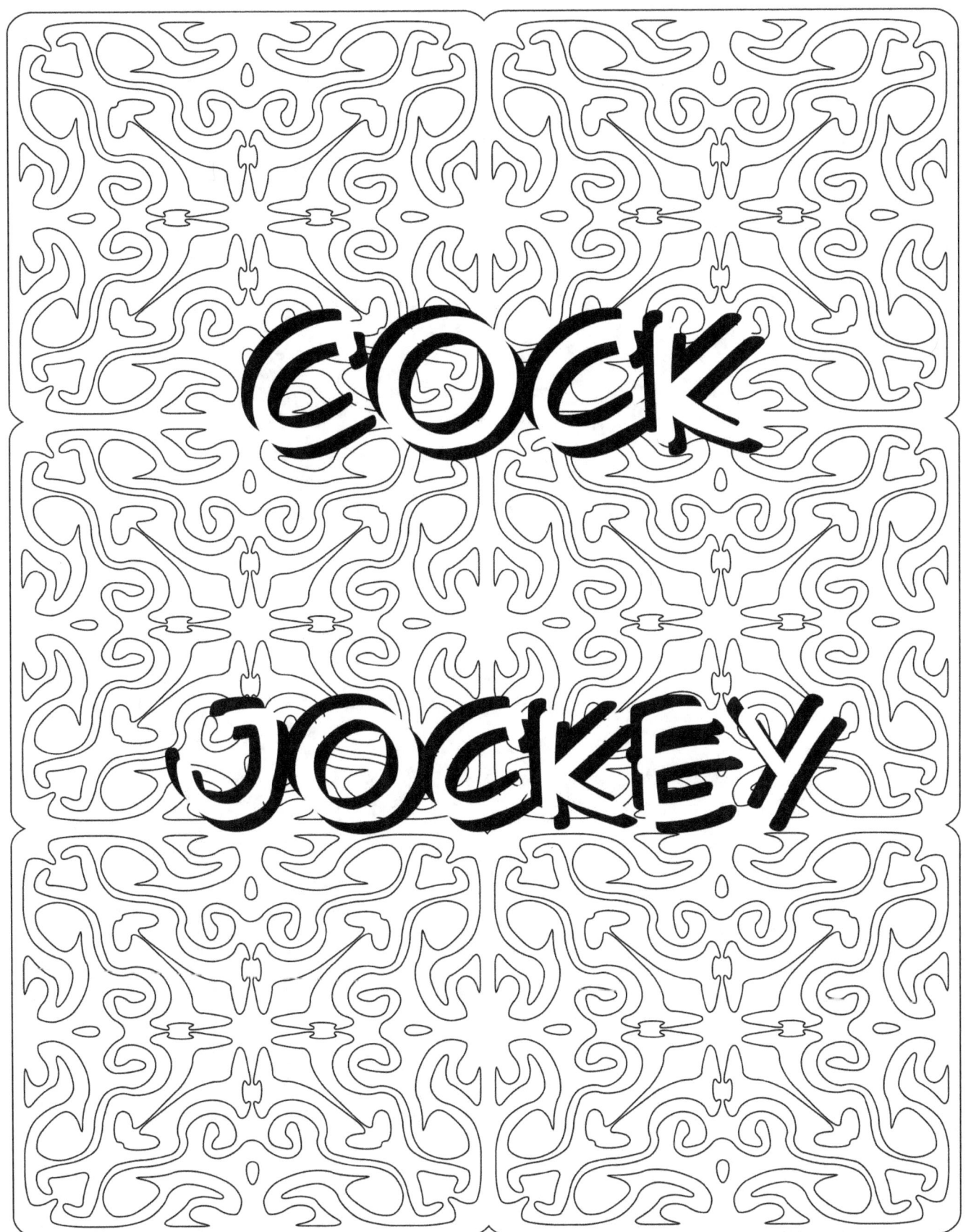

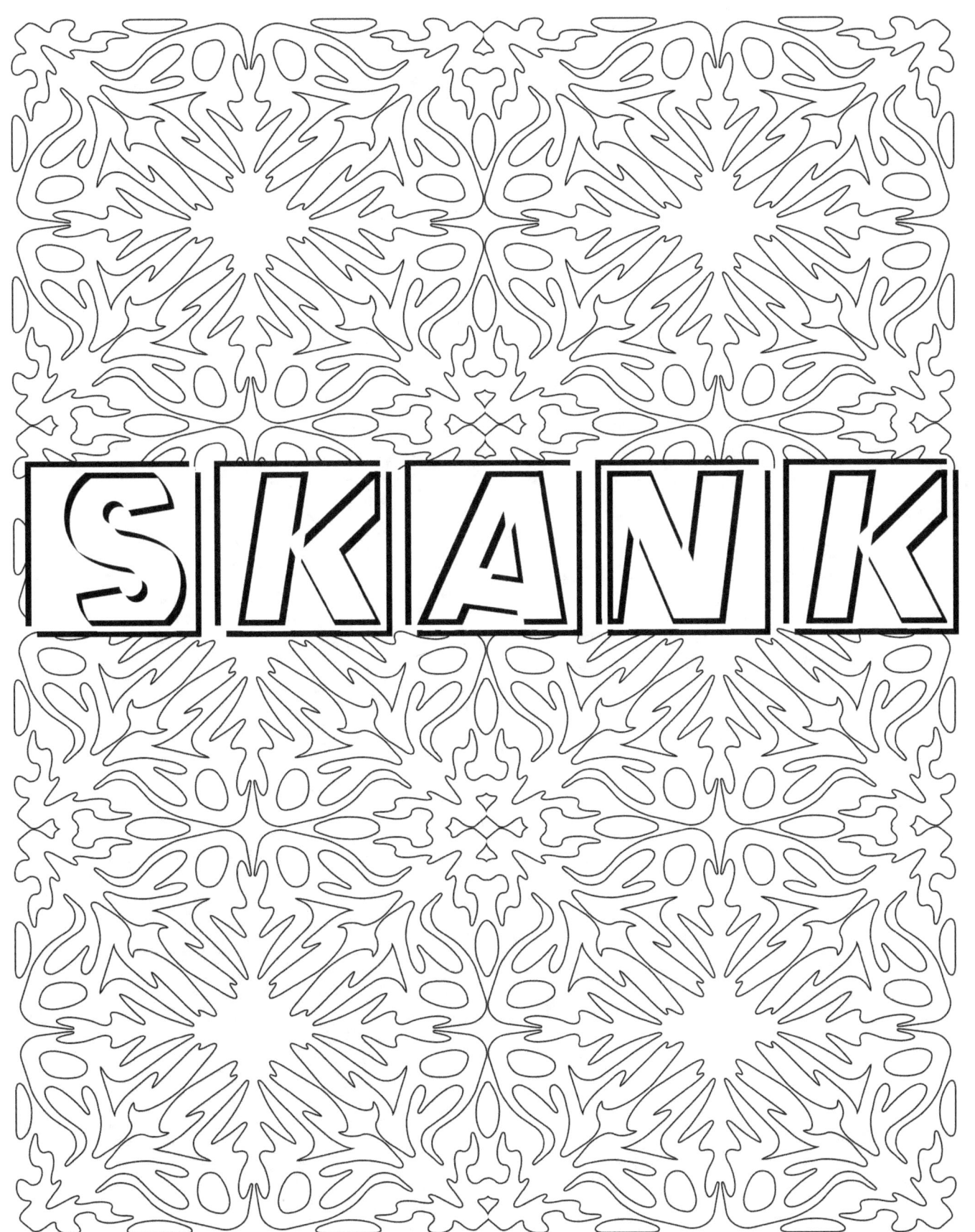

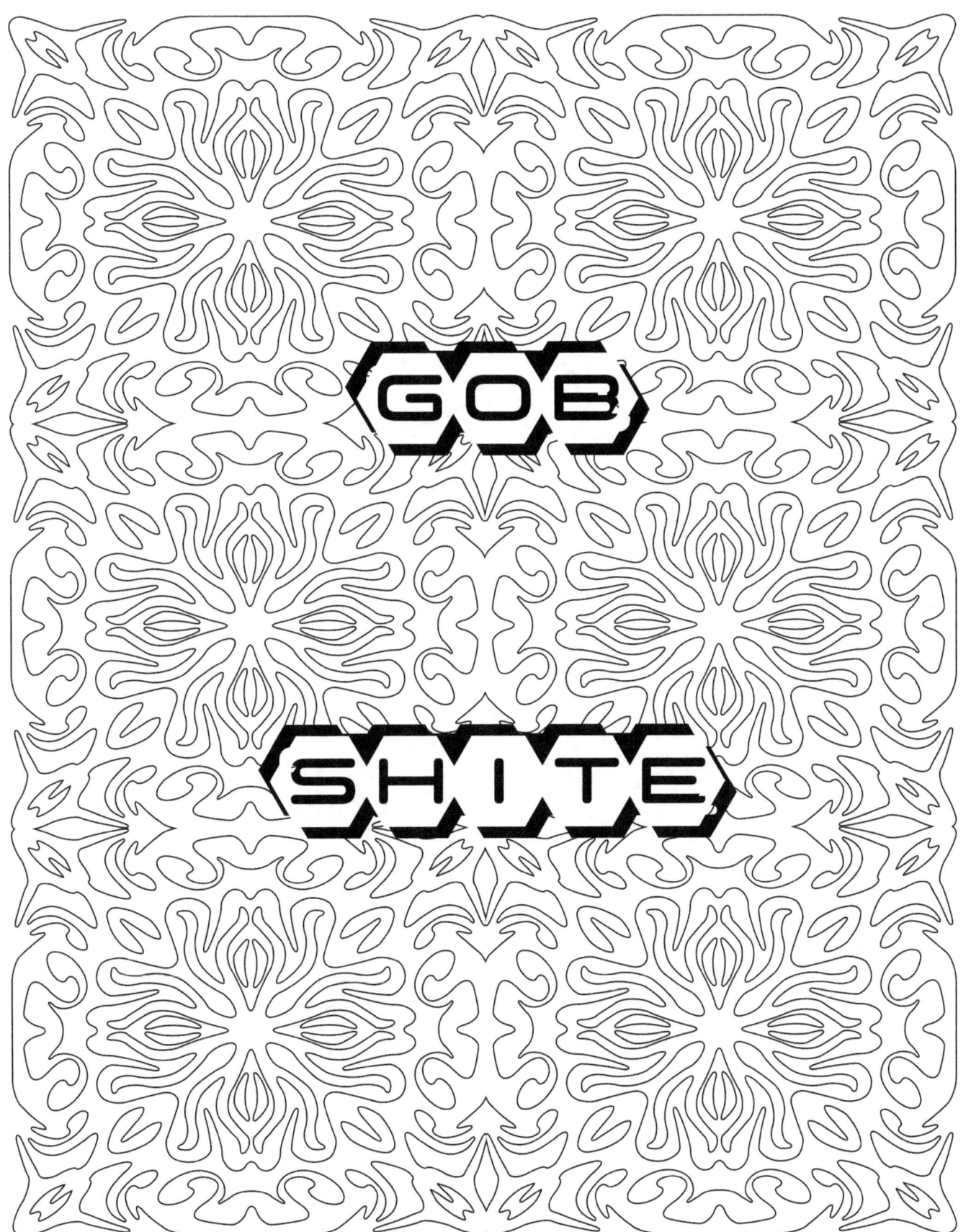

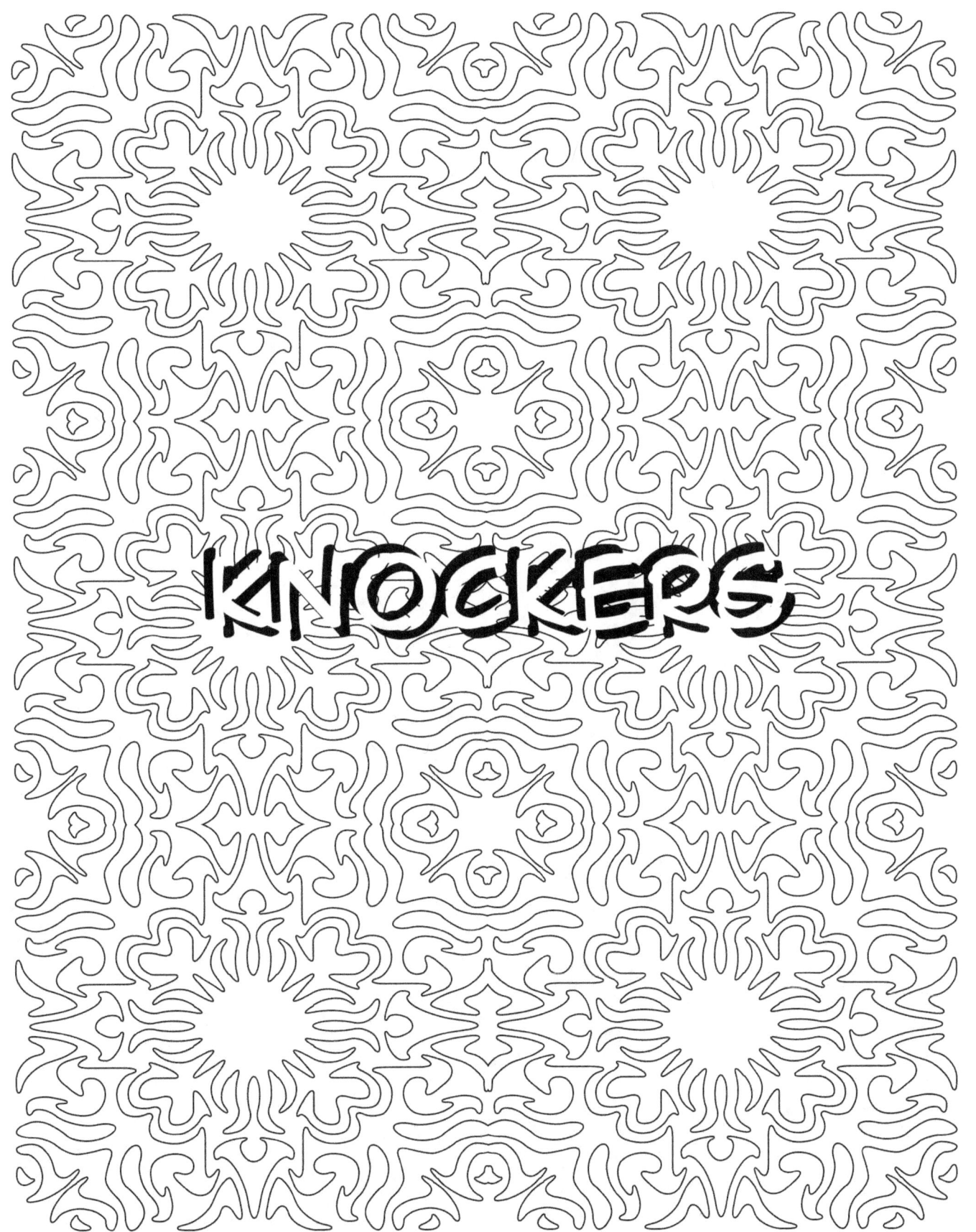

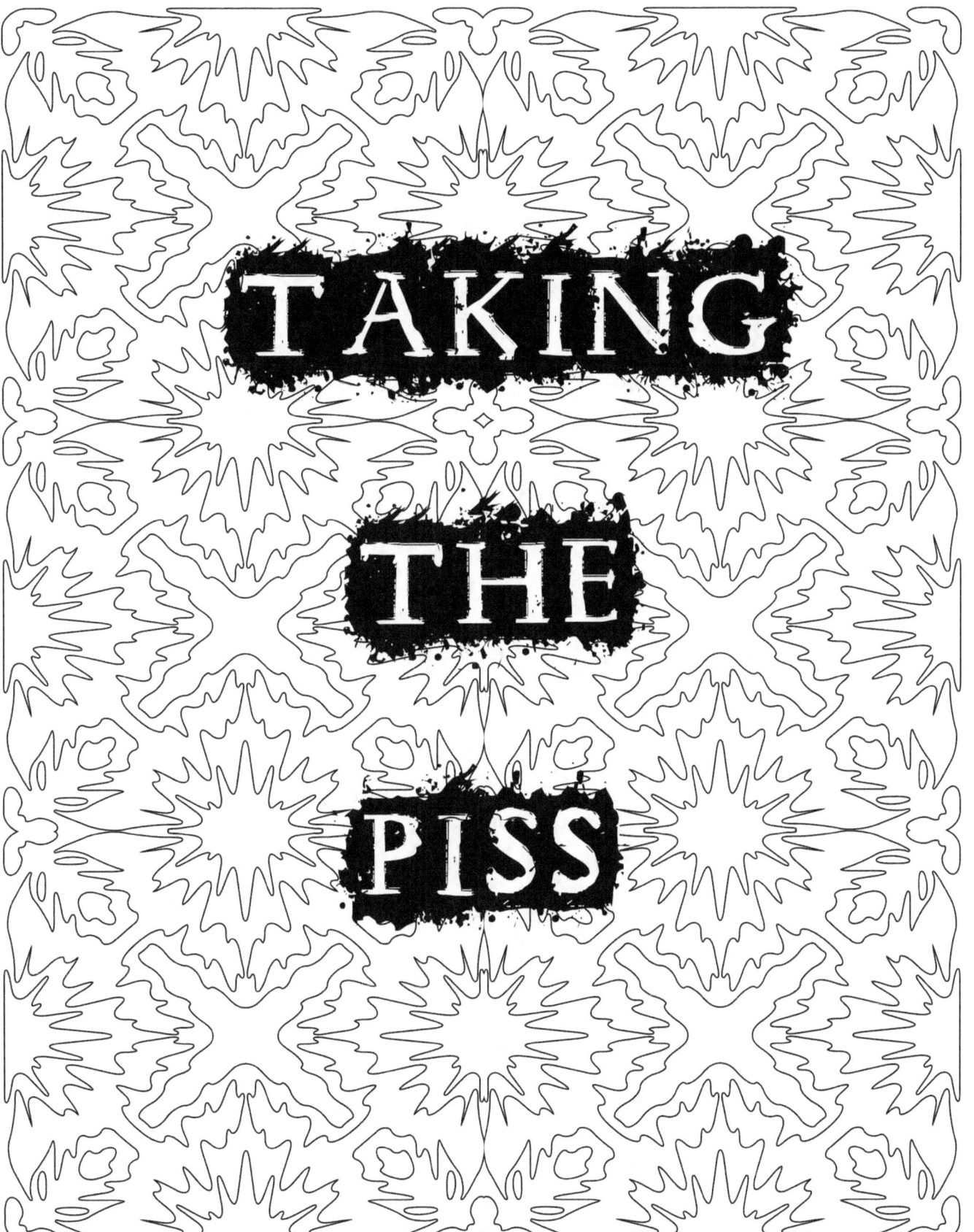

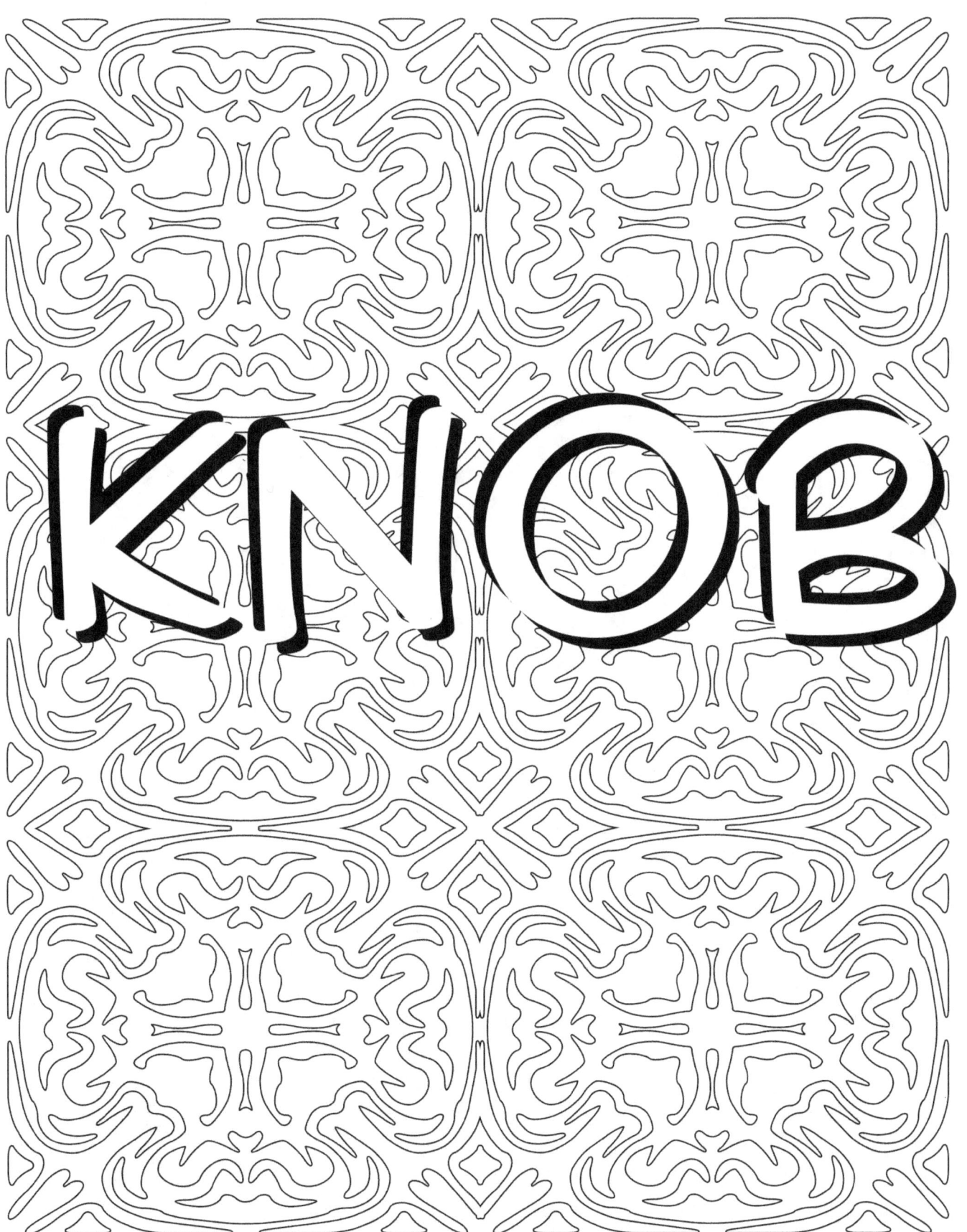

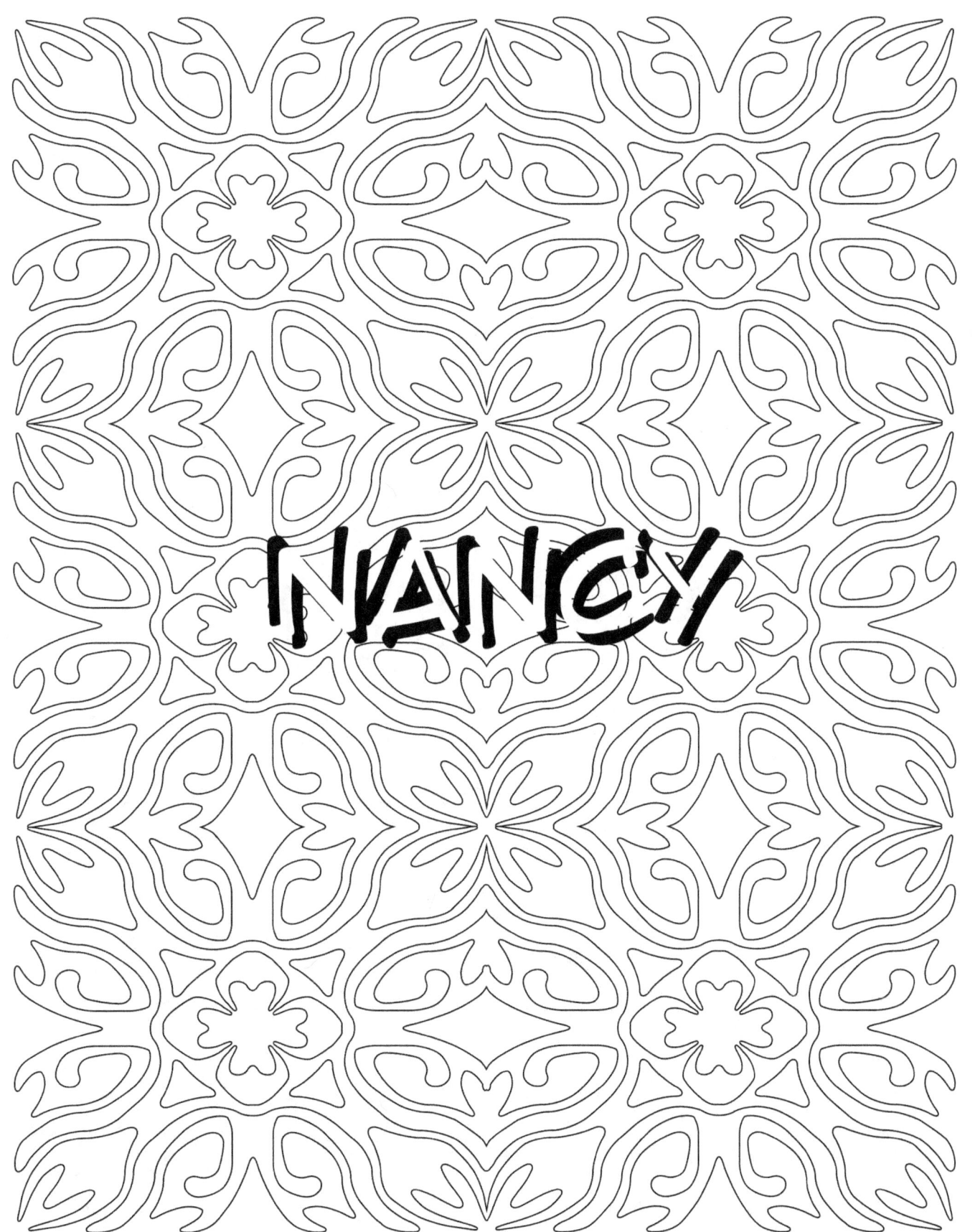

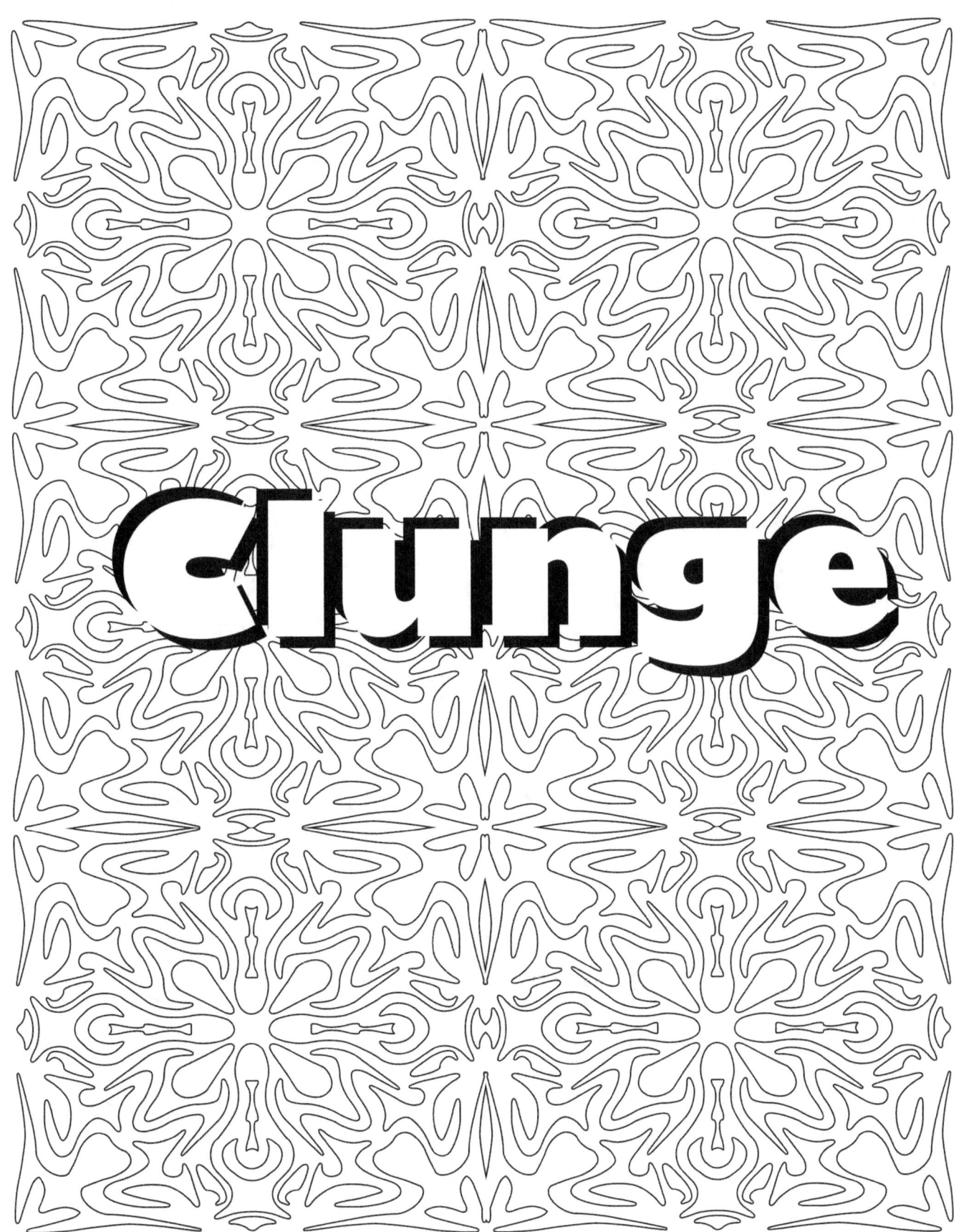

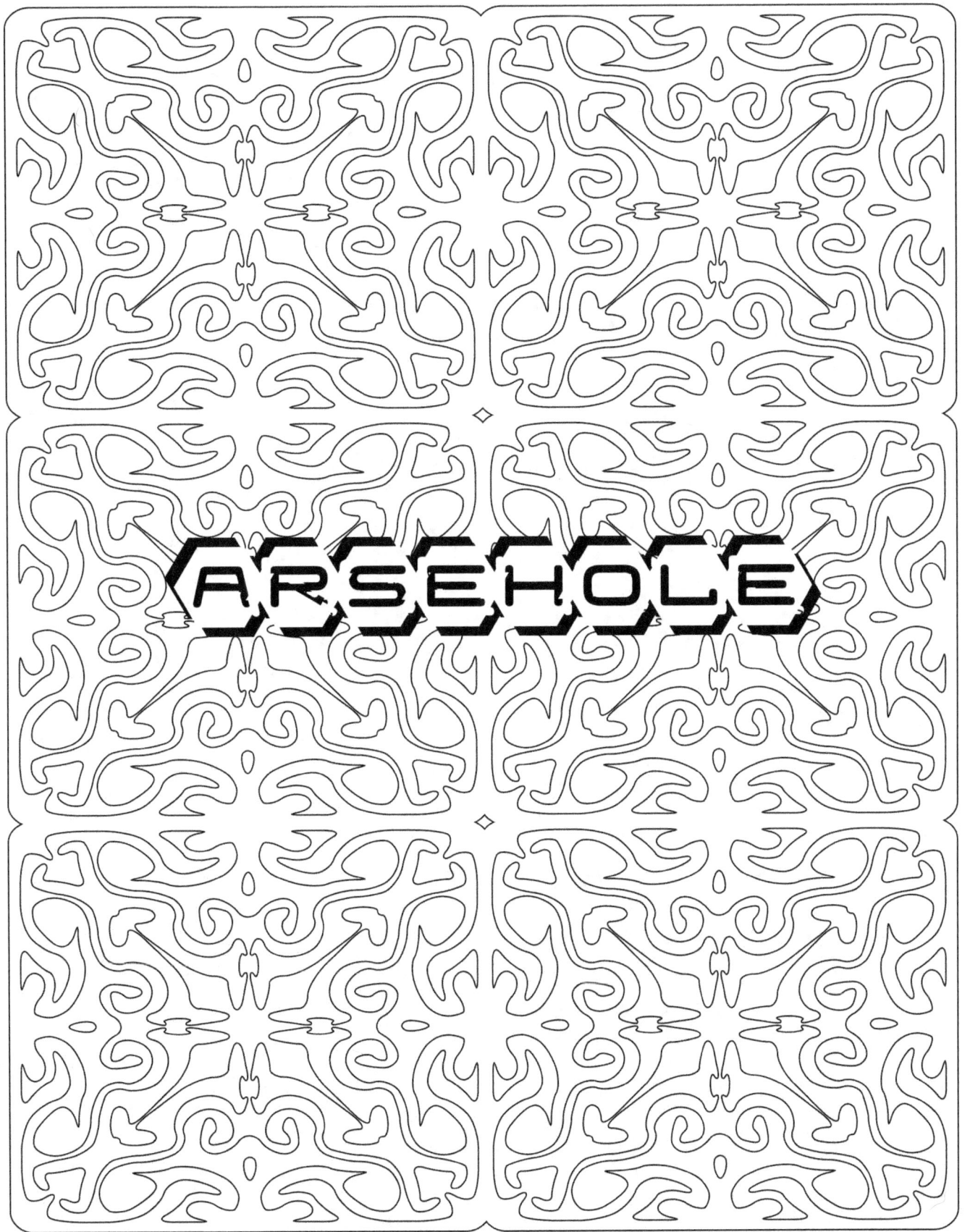

Final Words

Now Go Out There And Start Using Those Words!

Have Fun!